KENT FREE LIBRARY

```
J 979.2 Ay74
Ayres, B.
    Salt Lake City.
```

Salt Lake City

Salt Lake City
A Downtown America Book

Becky Ayres

d₽ Dillon Press, Inc. Minneapolis, MN 55415

Library of Congress Cataloging-in-Publication Data

Ayres, Becky.
　　Salt Lake City / Becky Ayres.
　　　　p.　　cm. — (A Downtown America book)
　　Summary: Describes the Utah capital, both past and present, providing information about neighborhoods, religion, attractions, festivals, people, industries, foods, life-style, historic sites, climate, and social concerns. Includes a brief history of the Mormon religion.
　　ISBN 0-87518-436-7 (lib. bdg)
　　1. Salt Lake City (UT)—Juvenile literature. [1. Salt Lake City (UT.)] I. Title. II. Series.
F834.S257A97　1990
979.2'258—dc 20　　　　　　　　　　　　　　90-2968
　　　　　　　　　　　　　　　　　　　　　　　　CIP
　　　　　　　　　　　　　　　　　　　　　　　　AC

© 1990 by Dillon Press, Inc. All rights reserved

Dillon Press, Inc., 242 Portland Avenue South
Minneapolis, Minnesota　55415

Printed in the United States of America
1　2　3　4　5　6　7　8　9　10　99　98　97　96　95　94　93　92　91　90

Acknowledgments

With thanks to Charles, Anne, and Beth Hickox; Jeanne Leigh Goldstein, Salt Lake City Convention and Visitors Bureau, the Utah State Historical Society, and the many others in Salt Lake who furnished information and pictures.
　　Photos have been provided by Keith Ayres, the Utah State Historical Society, the Salt Lake Convention and Visitors Bureau, Jeff Allred, George Karahalious, Beth Hickox, the Utah Heritage Foundation, and Carl Inoway.

Contents

City Flag.

	Fast Facts about Salt Lake City	6
1	A City in the Wilderness	11
2	Temple Square	21
3	Crossroads of the West	29
4	North, South, East, West	37
5	Having Fun	45
	Places to Visit in Salt Lake City	54
	Salt Lake City: A Historical Time Line	57
	Index	58

 City Seal.

Fast Facts about Salt Lake City

Salt Lake City: Mormon Capital; The New Jerusalem; City of the Saints; Crossroads of the West

Location: North central Utah, at the western foot of the Wasatch Mountains

Area: City, 75 square miles (194 square kilometers); metropolitan area, 2,099 square miles (5,436 square kilometers)

Population (1987 estimate*): City, 163,034; consolidated metropolitan area, 910,222

Major Population Groups: British, Scandinavian, German, Hispanic

Altitude: 4,220 feet (1,286 meters) above sea level

Climate: Average temperature is 37°F (3°C) in January, 88°F (31°C) in July; average annual precipitation is 69 inches (175 centimeters)

Founding Date: 1847, incorporated as a city in 1851

City Flag: A pioneer family, covered wagon, and two sea gulls in shades of blue and yellow on a white background, with the words, "This Is The Place, Salt Lake City"

City Seal: The Salt Lake City and County Building with the words, "Salt Lake City, Utah, Corporate Seal" around the rim

Form of Government: Mayor-Council; a mayor and seven council members are elected to 4-year terms

Important Industries: Mining, electronics, chemical and missile manufacturing, petroleum refining, transportation, banking, tourism

*Official 1990 U.S. Bureau of the Census figures available in 1991-92.

Festivals and Parades

January: Utah International Auto Show at the Salt Palace

May: Living Traditions: A Celebration of Salt Lake's Folk and Ethnic Arts at Liberty Park

June: Utah Slavia Festival at Old Mill; Utah Arts Festival at Triad Center

July: Days of '47 Celebration; Japanese Obon Festival

August: Swiss Independence Day Celebration at Sugarhouse Park; World Folk Festival at the Salt Palace; Utah Belly Dance Festival in Liberty Park

September/October: Greek Festival; Oktoberfest at Snowbird Ski and Summer Resort

November/December: Dickens Christmas Festival; Festival of the Trees at the Salt Palace; Lighting of Temple Square

For further information about festivals and parades, see the agencies listed on page 56.

United States

Salt Lake City

UTAH — Salt Lake City

N ↑

GREAT SALT LAKE

Wasatch National Forest

SALT LAKE CITY

INTERSTATE 15

Salt Lake City International Airport

SURPLUS CANAL

JORDAN RIVER

CITY CREEK

Riverside Park

MARMALADE DISTRICT

THE AVENUES

North Temple Street

South Temple Street

Interstate 80

Jordan Park

Liberty Park

State Street

Pioneer Trail State Park

SUGARHOUSE
Sugarhouse Park

Interstate 80

West Valley City

South Salt Lake

Points of Interest

1. Children's Museum
2. Utah State Capitol
3. Utah State Fair Grounds
4. Beehive House
5. Temple Square: Assembly Hall, Sea Gull Monument, the Temple, and the Tabernacle
6. Family History Library
7. Salt Palace
8. International Peace Gardens
9. Raging Waters
10. Utah Museum of Natural History
11. University of Utah
12. Fort Douglas Military Reserve
13. Hogle Zoo
14. This Is The Place Monument

0 miles 2½ 5
0 kilometers 4 12

A City in the Wilderness

Looking down on Salt Lake City from the nearby Wasatch Mountains, it is hard to imagine what the area looked like without a single building or tree. But take away the city and its suburbs so there is only the Great Salt Lake, the salt flats, and the gray Oquirrh Mountains beyond. This is what it looked like when Brigham Young led the Mormon pioneers here in 1847.

Now the Salt Lake Valley is the home of 700,000 people, and Salt Lake City, Utah, is the biggest city between Colorado and California. Located in the middle of the northern half of Utah, the city is about 75 miles (120 kilometers) south of the Idaho border. Unlike many other cities, Salt Lake was carefully planned before the first house was built. All the original streets run exactly north

The Wasatch Mountains tower over Salt Lake City to the east.

to south and east to west. The streets were also built wide enough for a team of oxen pulling a wagon to turn around. This has made it easier in modern times for Salt Lake to solve traffic and parking problems.

Salt Lake is also different from most major cities in another way. It does not have many tall buildings. There has been so much room to spread out in the valley that it has not been necessary to build high-rises.

The city's tallest building is the Mormon Church's office building. It is 28 stories high and has an observation deck near the top. Right across the street are Salt Lake's most well known buildings, the Mormon Temple and Tabernacle. These are in Temple Square at the heart of downtown Salt Lake City. The Temple's six soaring towers have been a landmark since 1893.

Salt Lake City borders the Great Salt Lake Desert, but it is not always hot here. June, July, and August have hot summer weather with temperatures near 88°F (31°C). September and October are sunny, but much cooler with an average high of 67°F (19°C).

Autumn is a favorite time for hiking and picnicking in the Wasatch Mountains. Winter also finds many Salt Lakers in the mountains, this time to ski at Alta, Snowbird, Park City, and other popular ski areas. Children can often go sledding and tubing in the city's parks. Spring brings rain and warmer weather, which melts the

The Mormon Temple is the focal point of Temple Square.

snow in the mountains and sometimes causes flooding.

The valley to the west of the city is bare and gray. Yet Salt Lake City itself is filled with trees, gardens, and grassy parks. The largest is Liberty Park, an 80-acre (32-hectare) area a few blocks from downtown. It has a pond, museum, aviary, and amusement park.

Another large area of grass and trees surrounds the Utah state capitol. Salt Lake City is the capital of Utah. The capitol building sits on a hill four steep blocks northeast of Temple Square. It looks like the nation's Capitol with its large, central dome.

Salt Lake City is also the county seat of Salt Lake County. Many residents work for the federal, state,

Skiing is often a family affair in areas close to Salt Lake City.

The Utah state capitol is made partly of Utah granite and has a copper dome.

county, and city governments. A large number of people also work for the mining, electronics, and defense industries located here, as well as for the many banks in the city. The largest employers in the area are the public schools and the University of Utah.

An important part of the university is the Health Sciences Center. It is a leader in developing artificial parts for the human body. Some people who have lost one of their own arms use the "Utah Arm." It can move and work much like a real arm. An artificial heart was also developed there. Researchers are now trying to create other artificial body parts, such as skin, nerves, and blood.

When Salt Lakers are not at work or school, there are dozens of things to do and places to visit. Theater, music, and dance have always been popular here. The Utah Symphony, Ballet West, and the Mormon Tabernacle Choir are famous all over the world. The University of Utah and the Salt Palace, a domed auditorium, host performances and sports events throughout the year. A dozen museums around the city display everything from dinosaur bones to race cars.

One attraction which has drawn Salt Lakers and tourists for many years is the Great Salt Lake. Until recently, it was almost as salty as the Dead Sea in the Mideast. The salt made it especially easy to float. People were able to bob around like corks with their hands and feet sticking up out of the water. Those with cuts or

People can no longer float in the Great Salt Lake as easily as these swimmers did several years ago.

Beehive House is one site that honors Salt Lake's Mormon heritage.

scrapes had to be brave because the extra-salty water really made them sting!

For the past few years, though, more water from the mountains has been running into the lake. This has made the lake bigger. It has also reduced the salt content in the lake. People still swim there, but now it is not any easier to float in the Great Salt Lake than it is in the ocean.

Salt Lake City is also known for its large Mormon population. It is called the "Mormon Capital" because it is the worldwide headquarters of that religion. Many places around the city honor this heritage. On the east side of the city is This Is The Place Monument and Pioneer Trail State Park. Original pioneer houses have been moved there from all over Utah. In the downtown area, a huge arch topped by an eagle spans State Street. This was once the entrance to Brigham Young's farm. There is no farm left, but his home, Beehive House, is open to the public.

For many years, the population of Salt Lake City was mostly Mormon. Even today, half the people who live here belong to that religion. Yet no matter which religion they follow, today's Salt Lakers take pride in their city's past, and work together to prepare for the future.

Temple Square

In the middle of downtown Salt Lake City is a 10-acre (4-hectare) square called Temple Square. It is the center of the Mormon religion. The full name for this group is the Church of Jesus Christ of Latter Day Saints, which is also called the LDS Church. Four million people a year admire the gardens, paintings, and sculptures in Temple Square.

Displays in the South Visitors' Center show how the LDS Church started in 1830 in New York. A young man named Joseph Smith told people that an angel showed him where to find a set of gold tablets, called *The Book of Mormon*. This book tells about a tribe of Israelites. The Mormons believe these people came to the Americas many centuries ago and became the American Indian tribes. Other paintings in the Visitors' Center show

Salt Lake City was built around Temple Square.

scenes of Smith organizing a religion based on that book. By 1833, he had convinced more than 1,000 people to join the LDS Church.

Other people, however, did not like this new religion. What they disliked most was the Mormons' belief in polygamy. This is the practice of being married to two or more women at the same time.

In 1838, the Mormons founded the town of Nauvoo, Illinois. Before settling there, they had already been forced to leave their homes in New York, Ohio, and Missouri. The people of Illinois did not welcome them, either. In 1844, Joseph Smith was killed by an angry mob of men who painted their faces so they would not be recognized.

The new Mormon leader, Brigham Young, decided that his people needed to find a place where no one else was living, and that no one wanted. After studying maps and talking to travelers, he chose the Salt Lake Valley. In the spring of 1847, Brigham Young left 3,000 Mormons at their winter camping place in Nebraska. A group of 143 men, 3 women, and 2 children traveled west with him, hoping to find a safe home. On July 24, they came through the last of the Wasatch Mountains. Brigham Young had been very sick, but he stood up in the wagon to look out over the empty Salt Lake Valley. "This is the right place," he said, "drive on."

Although the valley was dry and bare, the pioneers did not let it stay

This Is The Place Monument overlooks Salt Lake City from Emigration Canyon.

that way for long. By the end of the first week, they had built a dam and planted crops. In another few days, the site for the city was laid out, and the people began building a fort and houses. Because timber was hard to find, the pioneers learned to make bricks, called adobe, out of clay and straw. Most of the wall surrounding Temple Square today is made of these adobe bricks.

In September and October, 1,500 more Mormon pioneers arrived in the valley. Many of them survived the

Brigham Young.

winter by digging and eating the starchy root of the sego lily, which is now the state flower. Carvings of the lily can be seen on the organ in the Assembly Hall in Temple Square.

In the spring of 1848, more crops were planted, but frost killed some of them. Then one day, something even worse happened. Millions of black grasshoppers (or "Mormon crickets") appeared and began eating the remaining crops. For several days, the pioneers battled the insects, but without success. One morning, though, flocks of sea gulls arrived and ate enough grasshoppers to save the plants. Sea Gull Monument—topped by two gold-plated sea gulls—stands in Temple Square in honor of the state bird.

Salt Lake City grew quickly after

that first, hard year. Mormon missionaries went to other parts of the United States, and to some foreign countries to persuade people to accept the religion and move to Utah. For many years, most of the immigrants to Salt Lake City came from Great Britain and the Scandinavian countries. Today, many of the city's families are descendants of these early settlers.

The immigrants often arrived in Salt Lake City with no money. Near the Sea Gull Monument is a statue of a family struggling along with their handcart. It was built to honor the 4,000 pioneers who walked from Iowa to Utah because they could not afford an ox cart.

Although the early years were difficult, the pioneers still found the time and money to begin building a temple and a tabernacle. These are now the two main buildings in Temple Square.

The Tabernacle was completed in 1867. It was designed by a man who used his knowledge of bridgebuilding to design its rounded roof. The huge wooden arches are pinned with wooden pegs and rawhide thongs. The way the Tabernacle is built makes sound travel easily throughout the enormous building. A group of people seated in the back can hear a single pin dropped at the front, almost 50 yards (45 meters) away.

The organ in the Tabernacle is heard by radio all over the world. The original organ was built in 1866. Over the years, the organ has been rebuilt,

and today it has 11,623 pipes and five keyboards. There is a free recital every day. Twice a week, residents and visitors can also watch a rehearsal or performance of the Mormon Tabernacle Choir.

The biggest building in Temple Square is the Temple itself. One of the first things Brigham Young did when he arrived was to choose its location. Six years later, the settlers began building it. Slabs of granite were cut out of the mountains and hauled by ox cart to make the 16-foot (4.8-meter) thick walls. It took 40 years to complete the Temple. The general public may not enter the Temple, which is considered sacred. Only Mormons who live by the rules of the LDS Church may go inside.

Temple Square, though, is not just for Mormons. Many people working downtown stroll through the gates to rest on a shady bench and admire the beautiful gardens. The gardens are replanted for each season of the year. The square is truly the heart of the city, and Salt Lakers of all religions are proud of its history and beauty.

Temple Square tells only part of the Salt Lake story. Many people and events besides the LDS Church have helped form this city. It is younger than many other major American cities. Yet the pioneering spirit of its people, both past and present, has helped Salt Lake City grow in this unlikely place between the mountains and the desert.

The Mormon Tabernacle.

Crossroads of the West

No one paid much attention when the first settlers arrived in the Salt Lake Valley. The Ute, Paiute, Gosiute, and Shoshone Indian tribes who lived in Utah did not usually use that part of the region. The valley had been a part of a Spanish or Mexican territory for 200 years, but those countries never started settlements there.

English and American fur trappers explored Utah's Wasatch Mountains in the 1800s. In 1824, they discovered the Great Salt Lake. None of them thought that anyone would ever want to live in that harsh, uninviting land. According to legend, a famous mountain man named Jim Bridger even told Brigham Young he would pay him $1,000 for the first bushel of corn grown in the valley. The bushel of corn was grown, but the bet was never paid.

Original settlers' cabins have been moved to Pioneer Trail State Park.

From 1847 to 1849, the Mormon settlers lived without much contact with the rest of the United States. In 1849, though, a flood of hopeful miners passed through Salt Lake City on their way to the California gold mines. They were willing to pay high prices for supplies, and a number of businesses were started to sell them food and other goods. The area was helped further when Utah was made a U.S. territory in 1850.

In 1863, gold, silver, and copper were discovered in nearby Bingham Canyon. This brought the first large groups of non-Mormon settlers to the Salt Lake City area. Men were hired in Greece, Italy, and the Slavic countries of central Europe by work bosses who promised high wages. They told the miners that they would soon have enough money to return home as wealthy men. Instead, the miners were paid very little. Most of them finally decided to stay and save enough money to send for their families, or for brides picked out by relatives.

One of the first large mines was the Utah Copper Mine. It was the first open-pit copper mine in the world. Instead of digging tunnels to find ore, the miners dug a large pit, then kept making it deeper and wider. Kennecott Bingham Copper Mine, as it is called now, is still operating. Today, it is more than two miles (3.2 kilometers) wide and a half mile (.8 kilometer) deep. It is the largest mine of its kind in the United States.

Kennecott Bingham Copper Mine is the largest open-pit mine in the United States.

In 1869, the Union Pacific Railroad, which was building track from the east, and the Central Pacific, which was building from the west, came together in Utah. This was the first form of public transportation to cross the United States from ocean to ocean. Salt Lake City was now connected to the rest of the United States. It quickly became a transportation and trading center for the large area between the Rocky Mountains and the Sierra Nevada Mountains.

In 1896, Utah became the forty-fifth state. Since that time, Salt Lake and its suburbs have continued to grow. One of the biggest reasons for this growth is the natural resources in the area. During World War II, the metals and minerals found in the Salt Lake Valley became even more important than they had been. Mines and refineries grew much larger. Today, crude oil from southern Utah and neighboring states is shipped to Salt Lake City, where large plants refine it into gasoline. It is then sent by pipeline to other parts of the West.

Even the Great Salt Lake is "mined." Nearly 20,000 tons (18,000 metric tons) of common salt is taken out of the lake each year. This is done by pumping lake water into shallow pits or containers. After the sun has dried up the water, the salt is left at the bottom. People flying into or out of Salt Lake City International Airport often get a good view of this operation.

Salt Lake City's central location is important to many businesses. Big companies such as AT&T, Delta Air Lines, Kimberly-Clark, and American Express have regional or national offices in the area. Over the years, all these industries and businesses have attracted more people to Salt Lake City.

As in all cities, growth has brought problems along with change. Refineries and other industries have created jobs, but they have also caused air pollution. The growing number of cars adds to the problem. Salt Lake City has a large bus system, but with two interstate freeways and several expressways passing through the city, most people depend on cars. Sometimes the dirty air is trapped by the mountains and hangs over the valley for several days. The city has tried to control automobile fumes by requiring a yearly inspection of every car's exhaust system.

Salt Lake City also has a growing homeless population to care for. One way the Salt Lake City School District helps these people is by operating a special school for homeless children.

Some children attend the school for several months. Others go for just a few days until their parents move to another city. A special grant pays for the children's breakfasts, and a hot lunch is provided by the school. The teacher works with all ages, and older students help younger ones with their lessons. Students study the same subjects as other schoolchildren, but the teacher also spends a lot of time helping them learn how to make decisions and feel good about themselves.

A teacher helps a student at Salt Lake City's school for homeless children.

Salt Lake has also found a way to help some of its disabled residents. At ten busy downtown intersections, the city has installed special traffic lights so blind people can cross safely.

The lights give a "chirp" when it is safe to cross north-south, and a "cuckoo" when the light is green for east-west.

In 1983, Salt Lake City faced an unusual emergency. That year, heavy snowfalls in the winter created problems in the spring. The creeks and rivers which run from the mountains to the Great Salt Lake began to flood as the snow melted. For once, there was too much water. Thousands of volunteers built sandbag dikes next to streams and rivers. When the water kept rising, they also built dikes along

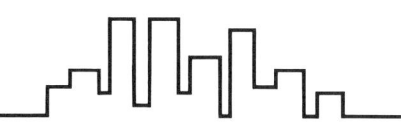

State Street in the middle of the city. The busy street became a river and kept the downtown area from being flooded.

All that water ran into the Great Salt Lake. The lake kept getting bigger because no rivers run out of it. Nearby roads and railroad tracks began disappearing under the water. This caused some disagreements between Salt Lakers. Some thought the lake's natural cycle of rising and falling should be left alone. Others felt too many roads and too much agricultural land would be lost if the lake continued to grow. Although it has been expensive, millions of gallons of water have been pumped out of the lake to keep it from getting larger.

Salt Lake City has changed in many ways since it was founded. It began as an all-Mormon farming community. Today it is a city where people of many religions work in all kinds of trades and businesses. Instead of an isolated town in the desert, Salt Lake City is now called "The Crossroads of the West."

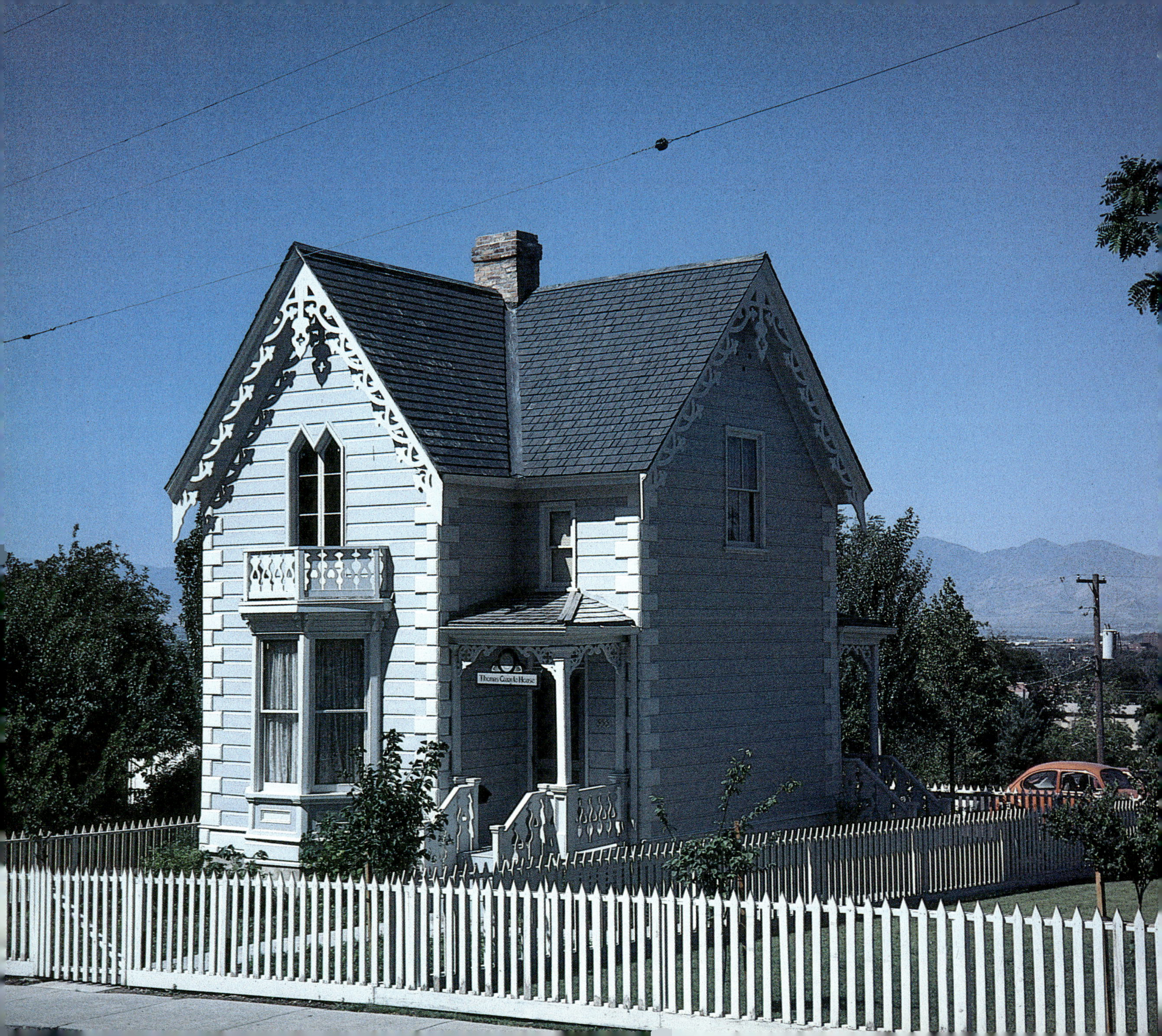

North, South, East, West

The orderly pattern of streets that starts in downtown Salt Lake makes it easy to find addresses around much of the city and its suburbs. Most of the streets have numbers and directions in their names, such as 600 East. The numbering system starts at the southeast corner of Temple Square. A street named 200 West will be two blocks west from that point. A street named 4500 South will be 45 blocks south. Residents often give directions by saying "turn east" or "go two blocks north" instead of saying "left" and "right."

One of the neighborhoods without numbered streets is called the Marmalade District. It is near the capitol. Streets here are named after fruits, such as Quince and Apricot. This area contains restored homes from the early 1900s when mine owners and businesspeople built large, fancy houses.

This house on Quince Street in the Marmalade District is one of the few wooden frame houses from the 1880s.

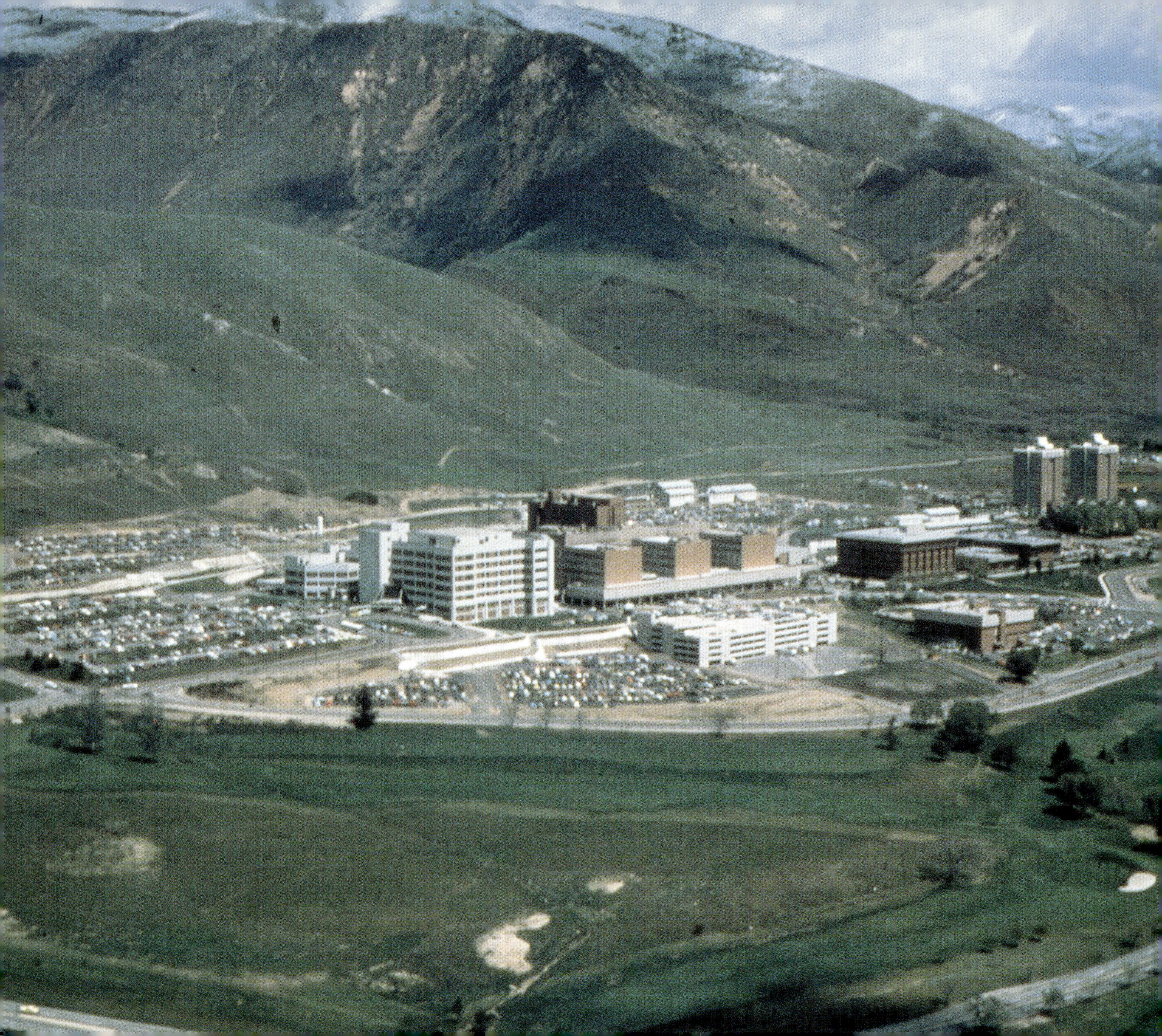

Another nearby area is called the Avenues. The houses in the Avenues were also built 80 or 90 years ago. They are near the University of Utah. Over the years, many were turned into apartments for students. Now, though, some of these homes are being restored by young professional families to look as they did originally.

The east side of the city is called the Benches. Thousands of years ago, the valley was covered by a freshwater lake. As the level of the lake's water became lower, it cut ledges, or benches, into the sides of the hills and mountains. The University of Utah and many beautiful homes are built in these bench areas overlooking the whole valley.

Another part of Salt Lake City with its own name is Sugarhouse. Before the railroad came to the city, it was hard to get sugar. The settlers built a refinery where they tried to make their own sugar out of carrots and other vegetables. Their plan did not work. Today, Sugarhouse is a busy area of stores, homes, and apartments.

The Salt Lake City metropolitan area is made up of Salt Lake City and several smaller suburbs. These are connected to the city on the south and west. Many of their residents commute to jobs in Salt Lake City. The capital is also a short distance from Ogden, one of Utah's other major cities. Many Ogden residents make the 30-mile (48-kilometer) drive into Salt Lake to work.

At one time, small sections of Salt

The University of Utah campus sits on benches formed by Lake Bonneville thousands of years ago.

Young Salt Lakers take part in the annual Greek Festival.

Lake City were filled with homes and businesses of people from a particular country. The families of Greek, Japanese, and Slavic laborers lived in the southwest section of downtown. Today, their churches, such as the Greek Orthodox Church and the Buddhist Temple, still serve city residents.

These ethnic groups no longer live all together in one area, or speak their grandparents' language. Many of them, though, sponsor festivals to celebrate their heritage and share it with others. The largest of these celebra-

Dancers of all ages fill the street for the Obon Festival.

tions is the Greek Festival. It is held the first week in September. Nearly 50,000 people gather to enjoy Greek food, dancing, and crafts.

Another popular festival is the Slavia Festival. Held on Father's Day weekend, it brings together families from small mining communities throughout the state. During the Japanese Obon Festival, a whole street is closed to make room for the many dancers and visitors. There is a Swiss Independence Day celebration in Sugarhouse Park, a German Oktoberfest

Many buildings in downtown Salt Lake City are made from bricks.

at Snowbird Ski Resort, and several other folk festivals.

The largest minority group in Salt Lake City today is Hispanic. The Guadalupe Center on 600 West offers classes and services to many of the valley's 30,000 Hispanic residents. In recent years, Southeast Asians have immigrated to Salt Lake City, too. This group still makes up only 2 percent of the population, while the black community makes up less than 1 percent.

Despite their differences in age and wealth, nearly all of the neighborhoods in Salt Lake City are alike in some ways. One thing they have in common is brick. Unlike the early years, the Salt Lake Valley now has plenty of fruit and shade trees. Trees grown for lumber are still rare, though. About two-thirds of the houses and other buildings are built of brick, just as the first houses were. Luckily, the people no longer have to make their own!

There are also many children throughout Salt Lake City. Mormon families are often large. Nearly a third of the population of Salt Lake County is less than 15 years old. More than 160,000 students attend school in four districts. The Jordan District has so many students that some of its elementary schools run year-round. Students are divided into four groups. Three groups fill the classrooms, while one group takes a three-week vacation. In this way, each student gets a break after nine weeks of class.

Salt Lakers take pride in the neat and clean appearance of their city. The downtown area, with its modern malls and historic sites, bustles with businesspeople, shoppers, and tourists. Most neighborhoods throughout the city are well-kept and quiet. One of the things Salt Lakers enjoy most about living here is being able to use and enjoy nearly every part of their interesting city.

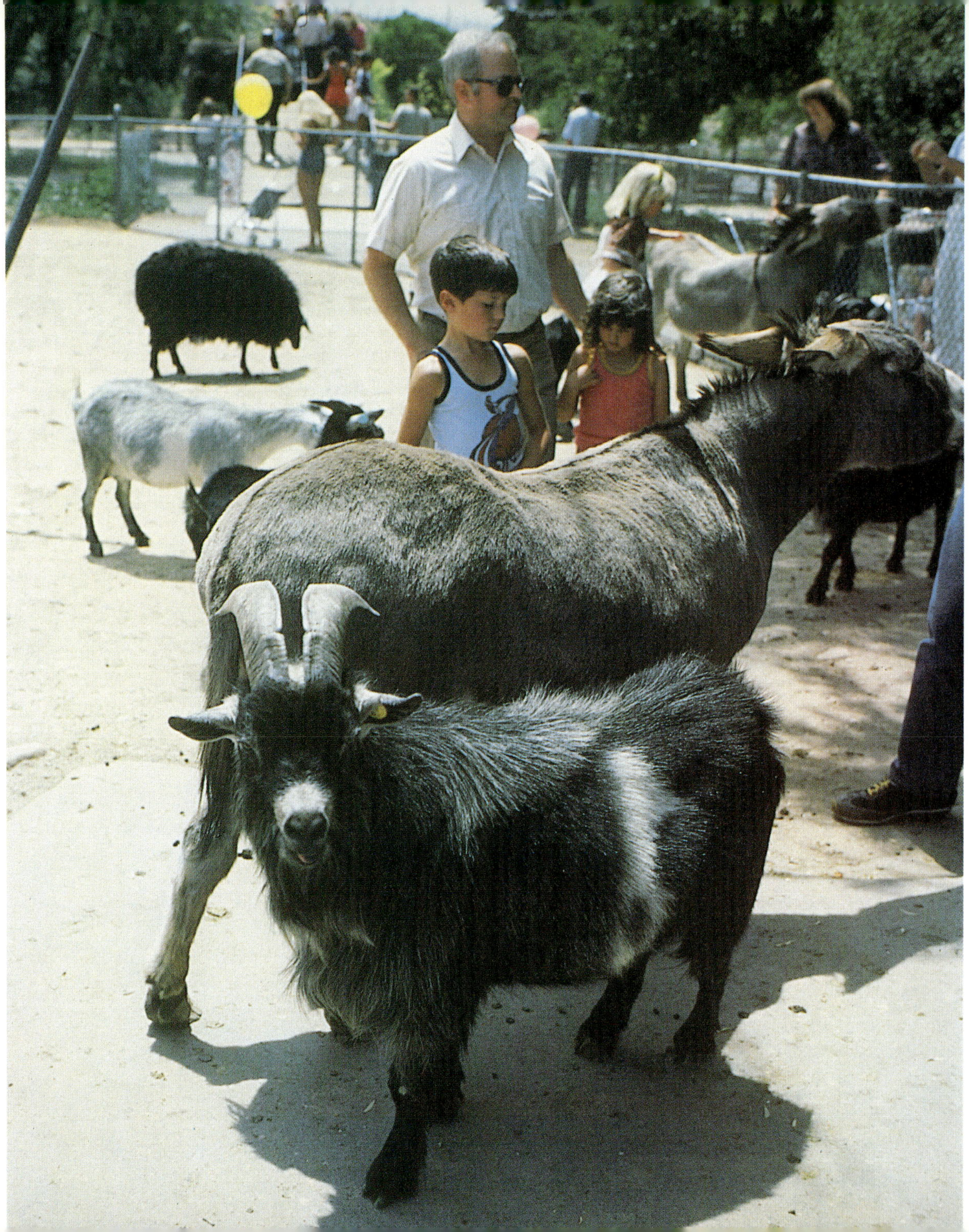

Having Fun

Family life is very important to Salt Lakers. The city offers many activities for families. One of the most popular is a visit to Hogle Zoo in Emigration Canyon. The zoo has more than 1,000 animals and special summer programs for people of all ages.

Another place to learn about animals is the Tracy Aviary in Liberty Park. Hundreds of birds, both common and unusual, live in this 11-acre (4.4-hectare) area which visitors can walk through. In the summertime, there are special bird shows. Birdwatchers can also visit the observation deck in the old Hotel Utah downtown. Here, they can see nests of peregrine falcons. Scientists brought the falcons to Salt Lake and several other cities. They hope that the birds will survive and increase their numbers in urban areas.

Visitors enjoy the petting zoo at Hogle Zoo.

Dinosaur skeletons found in Utah are displayed at the Utah Museum of Natural History.

The Utah Museum of Natural History at the University of Utah exhibits animals from the past and present. The most popular of these is the dinosaur bones. Four dinosaur skeletons from various parts of Utah are on display. The Museum of Natural History also holds family field trips, children's activities, and is the home of the Junior Science Academy.

Another place to have fun learning about nature is the Hansen Planetarium. Star shows, star parties, and laser light shows introduce families to the wonders of the universe.

The Children's Museum of Utah is located in a building built in the 1920s, but the exhibits are all about modern technology. In this "hands-on" museum, visitors can pilot a jet, perform an artificial heart operation, broadcast a news program, and try many other experiments.

The Salt Lake area has plenty of places to step into the past as well as the future. Residents and visitors alike can see what it was like to grow up on a farm 100 years ago at the Wheeler Farm in Murray, Utah. Young people, as well as adults, can feed the chickens, gather eggs, and milk the cows. Men and women dressed in costumes offer the weary workers a glass of lemonade and a slice of bread baked on a

Children enjoy a wagon ride at Wheeler Farm.

wood stove. Visitors can also go on a hayride, listen to stories, and watch how people did a variety of other things on an 1800s frontier farm.

The Pioneer Trail State Park near Hogle Zoo is the home of the This Is The Place Monument. It is also the site of a village where pioneer skills are shown. On special occasions, such as July 4 and Labor Day, children can try some of the crafts and chores.

A place where you may be able to learn about your own family's past is the Mormon Family History Library. The library staff will help you find records of births, marriages, deaths, and other information about your ancestors. The library has records of 2 billion people who were born before 1900.

Salt Lakers enjoy all kinds of sports—whether they are watching them or taking part in them. The National Basketball Association's Utah Jazz basketball team fills the Salt Palace with fans for each game. The Golden Eagle professional hockey team also plays at the Salt Palace. Baseball fans support Salt Lake's minor league team, the Salt Lake Trappers.

The Bonneville Speedway lies west of the city on the salt flats. Since 1914, race car drivers have been setting many world records for speed there. Photographs of the speedway and a record-breaking car from 1936, the *Mormon Meteor*, are on display in the basement of the capitol.

When most people think of sports in Salt Lake City, they think of skiing.

It is a very popular pastime. But the city offers plenty of other sporting activities, too. In the summer, Salt Lakers take advantage of the many tennis courts, golf courses, and swimming pools. A popular place on hot days is Raging Waters, a water park with 11 pools and 17 water slides. Since 1896, Salt Lakers have been visiting an amusement and swimming park called Lagoon, 15 miles (24 kilometers) north of the city.

For indoor fun in any weather, families and young people head for the 49th Street Galleria in Murray. This is one of the largest entertainment malls in the nation. It has bowling, roller skating, batting cages, miniature golf, games, food, live entertainment, and special events.

The Utah Jazz provides basketball excitement at the Salt Palace.

From pioneer days to the present, the Salt Lake Valley residents have loved music, dance, and theater. One of the most popular ballet productions each year is the Christmastime performance of *The Nutcracker*. Salt Lakers are also proud of their symphony, modern dance troupe, and opera company.

A popular theater event every summer is the production of *Promised Valley*. This musical play about the Utah pioneers is performed in July and August in a restored nineteenth-century playhouse downtown. In addition, the Pioneer Theatre Company at the University of Utah and the Salt Lake Repertory Theatre produce plays for children as well as adults.

Salt Lakers of any age look forward to the city's biggest yearly celebration. The "Days of '47" festivities begin early in July and continue through Pioneer Day on July 24. One of the events, the Youth Parade, is the largest parade of children in the country. More than 4,000 costumed children march along with bands, clowns, and 80 miniature floats. Other events include another parade, a giant rodeo, concerts, and races.

Summer closes with the Utah State Fair in early September. Carnival rides, livestock, entertainers, food and craft booths, and a rodeo attract people to the fairgrounds from all over the state.

During December, parents bundle up the family to walk around Temple Square. Each night, from Thanksgiving until New Year's Day, the square sparkles with 300,000 tiny Christmas

The Days of '47 Parade.

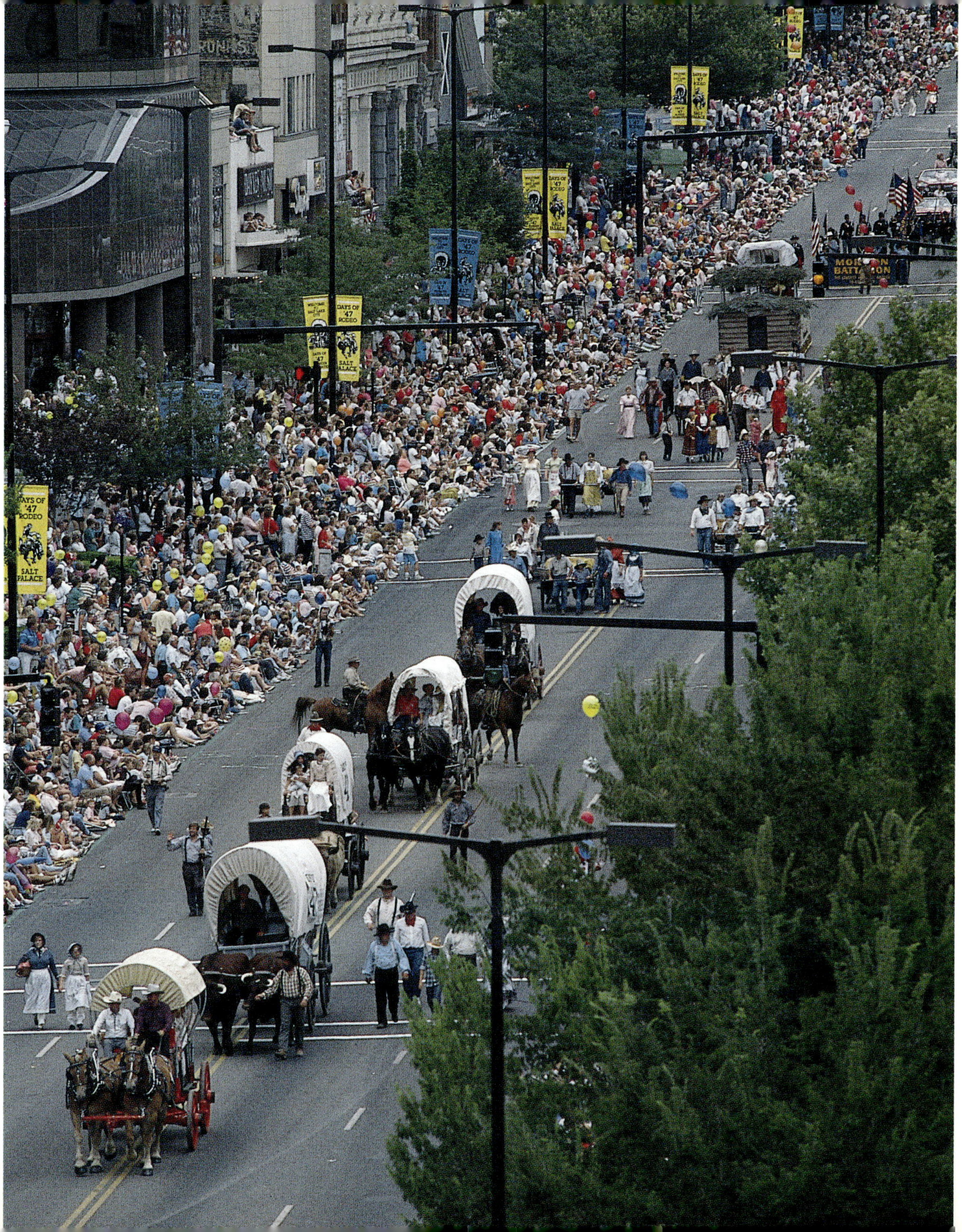
DAYS OF '47 RODEO
SALT PALACE

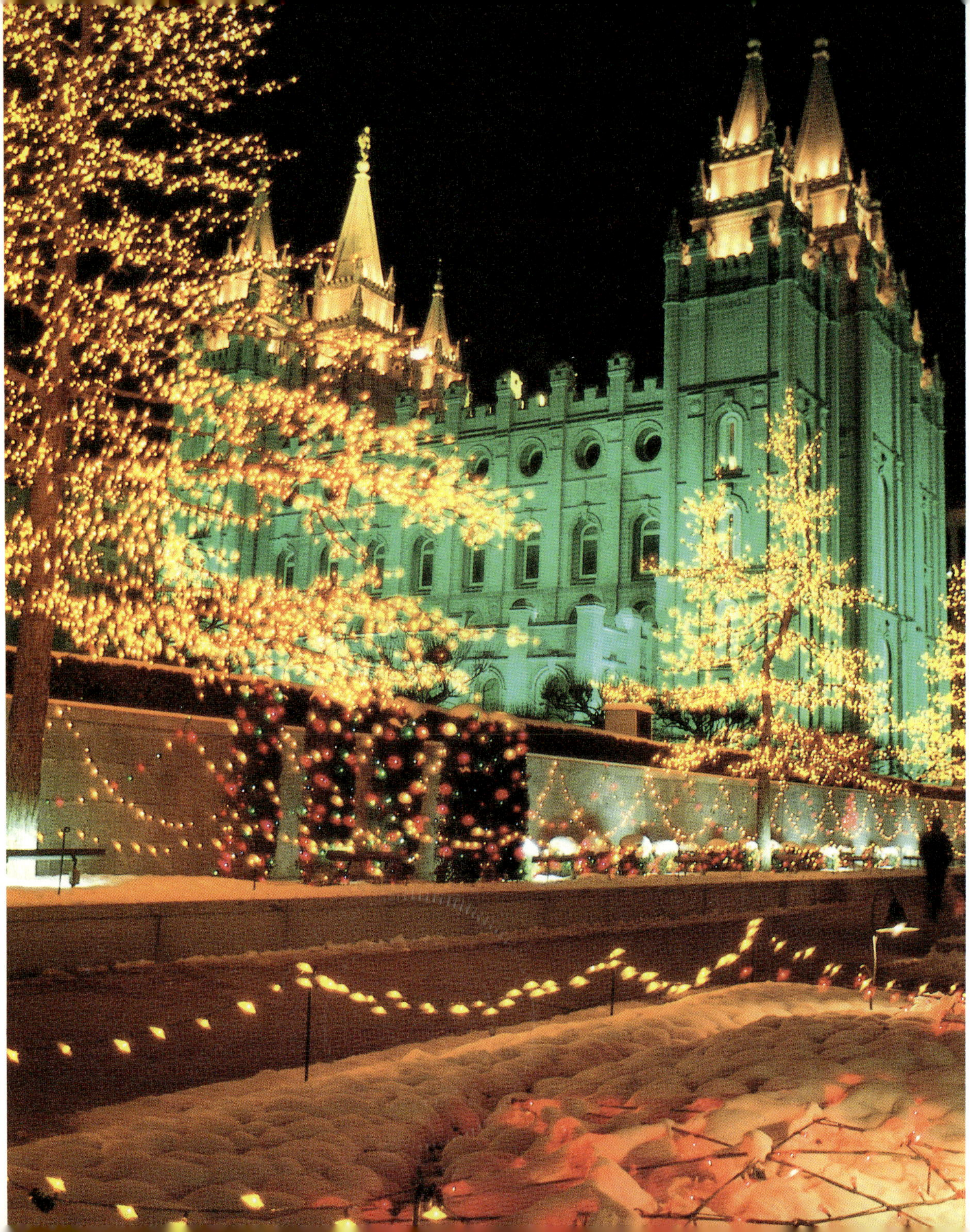

lights strung through every tree and bush. Salt Lakers and visitors enjoy the display—even though the temperatures are often below freezing!

Although Salt Lake City will probably grow and change along with its many children, the spirit that helped build it will remain the same. People whose families helped settle the valley welcome the more recent residents. Together, they try to keep Salt Lake City a good place to live, work, and play—now, and in the future.

Temple Square glitters with tiny lights during the Christmas season.

Places to Visit in Salt Lake City

Historical Museums and Sites

Beehive House
67 East South Temple
(801) 240-2671

Daughters of the Utah Pioneers Museum
300 North Main
(801) 538-1050
Thirty-seven rooms of pioneer objects

Museum of Church History and Art
45 North West Temple
(801) 240-2299

Pioneer Trail State Park
2602 East Sunnyside Avenue
(801) 533-5881

Temple Square
50 West South Temple
(801) 240-2534
Tours, concerts, and displays about the LDS Church

Utah Historical Society
300 Rio Grande
(801) 533-7037

Utah State Capitol Building
Capitol Hill at North State Street
(801) 538-3000

Wheeler Farm
6351 South 900 East
(801) 264-2212

Science and Nature

Children's Museum of Utah
840 North 300 West
(801) 322-5268

Hansen Planetarium
15 South State Street
(801) 538-2098

Hogle Zoo
2600 East Sunnyside Avenue
(801) 582-1631

Utah Museum of Natural History
University of Utah
(801) 581-4303

Parks

International Peace Gardens
900 West 1000 South
A variety of gardens representing 14 different nations

Lagoon
Interstate 15 at Farmington
(801) 451-0101

Liberty Park
900 South 700 East
(801) 596-5034

Raging Waters
1200 West 1700 South
(801) 973-6600

Utah State Arboretum
University of Utah
(801) 581-7200

Fine and Performing Arts

Capitol Theater
50 West 200 South
(801) 538-2253

Promised Valley Playhouse
132 South State Street
(801) 364-5696

Salt Lake Art Center
20 South West Temple
(801) 328-4201

Symphony Hall
123 West South Temple
(801) 533-6407

Utah Museum of Fine Art
University of Utah
(801) 581-7332

Other Places to Visit

Family History Library
35 North West Temple
(801) 240-2331

Kennecott Copper Mine
Bingham Canyon
(801) 322-7260

LDS Church Office Building
60 East North Temple
(801) 240-2452

Salt Palace
100 South West Temple
(801) 363-6781

Additional information can be obtained from the following agency:

Salt Lake Visitor Information Center
180 South West Temple
Salt Lake City, Utah 84101-1493
(801) 521-2868

Salt Lake City: A Historical Time Line

1847	Brigham Young founds Great Salt Lake City
1849	California Gold Rush brings non-Mormons through Salt Lake City
1850	Utah Territory is formed; University of Deseret (later the University of Utah) is founded
1851	Great Salt Lake City is incorporated
1853	Work begins on LDS Temple in Salt Lake
1863	Valuable metals are discovered in Bingham Canyon
1868	The "Great" is dropped from Salt Lake City's name
1869	The transcontinental railroad is completed
1881	The first electric lights are installed in Salt Lake City
1890	The Mormon Church officially stops practicing polygamy
1893	The LDS Temple is completed
1896	Utah becomes the 45th state in the Union, and the fourth to extend voting rights to women
1916	The Utah state capitol is completed
1969	The Salt Palace opens
1979	Symphony Hall opens
1980	The mayor-council form of government is adopted
1982	An artificial heart is implanted in Barney Clark at the University Hospital
1986	The Great Salt Lake reaches its highest recorded level
1989	Scientists at the University of Utah announce a major breakthrough in experiments to create power through nuclear fusion; the state votes to improve winter sports facilities in Salt Lake City in the hopes of hosting a future winter olympics

Index

Beehive House, 19
Bingham Canyon, 30
Bonneville Speedway, 49
Book of Mormon, The, 21
Bridger, Jim, 29
Church of Jesus Christ of Latter Day Saints: beliefs of, 22; children and, 43; formation of, 21, 22; founding of Salt Lake City and, 22-24; missionaries and, 25; names for, 21; number in Salt Lake City of, 19
dance, 16, 50
education, 33, 43
Emigration Canyon, 45
festivals, 40-42, 53
Great Salt Lake, 11, 16, 18, 29, 32, 35
Great Salt Lake Desert, 13
Hogle Zoo, 45, 48
industry, 16, 30, 32-33
Kennecott Bingham Copper Mine, 30
Liberty Park, 15, 45
Mormons. *See* Church of Jesus Christ of Latter Day Saints
"Mormon Crickets," 24
Mormon Family History Library, 48
Mormon Tabernacle, 13, 25, 26
Mormon Tabernacle Choir, 16, 27
Mormon Temple, 13, 27
museums, 16, 27
music, 16, 50
Nauvoo, Ill., 22

neighborhoods, 37, 39
Nutcracker, The, 50
Oquirrh Mountains, 11
Pioneer Trail State Park, 18, 48
Promised Valley, 50
Rocky Mountains, 32
Salt Lake City: appearance of, 13, 15; children in, 43; climate of, 13, 15; flooding in, 34-35; geography of, 11; growth of, 25, 32; homeless people in, 33; homes in, 43; location of, 11; mining in, 30, 32; native Americans in, 29; nicknames for, 18, 35; people of, 25, 30, 42; pollution in, 33; railroads and, 32; settlers of, 11, 30; size of, 11; as a state capital, 15; streets in, 11, 13, 37
Salt Lake County, 15
Salt Palace, 16, 48
Sea Gull Monument, 24
Sierra Nevada Mountains, 32
skiing, 13
Smith, Joseph, 21, 22
sports, 48-49
Temple Square, 13, 21, 23, 24, 25, 27, 50-53
theater, 16, 50
This Is The Place Monument, 18, 48
Tracy Aviary, 45
University of Utah, 16, 39
Wasatch Mountains, 11, 13, 22, 29
World War II, 32
Young, Brigham, 11, 19, 23-24, 27, 29

About the Author

Becky Ayres is a media specialist and freelance writer whose work has appeared in a number of national magazines, including *The Mother Earth News* and *Child Life*. Although she is currently living in Oregon with her husband and daughter, Ayres grew up in the Salt Lake City area, and returns there whenever possible.

Reinforced Binding

00111 0991